Barking & Biting
The Poetry of Sina Queyras

Barking & Biting
The Poetry of Sina Queyras

Selected
with an
introduction by
Erin Wunker
and an
afterword by
Sina Queyras

LAURIER POETRY SERIES

WILFRID LAURIER
UNIVERSITY PRESS

Wilfrid Laurier University Press acknowledges the support of the Canada Council for the Arts for our publishing program. We acknowledge the financial support of the Government of Canada through the Canada Book Fund for our publishing activities. This work was supported by the Research Support Fund.

Library and Archives Canada Cataloguing in Publication

Queyras, Sina, 1963–
[Poems. Selections]
    Barking & biting : the poetry of Sina Queyras / selected with an introduction by Erin Wunker and an afterword by Sina Queyras.

(Laurier poetry series)
Includes bibliographical references.
Issued in print and electronic formats.
ISBN 978-1-77112-216-0 (paperback).—ISBN 978-1-77112-218-4 (epub).—
ISBN 978-1-77112-217-7 (pdf)

    i. Wunker, Erin, 1979–, editor   ii. Title.   iii. Title: Barking and biting.   iv. Title: Poems. Selections.   v. Series: Laurier poetry series

PS8533.U3414A6 2016   C811'.6   C2015-907849-0   C2015-907850-4

Front-cover photo by Sina Queyras. Cover design and text design by P.J. Woodland.

This book is printed on FSC® certified paper and is certified Ecologo. It contains post-consumer fibre, is processed chlorine free, and is manufactured using biogas energy.

Printed in Canada

MIX
Paper from
responsible sources
FSC® C004071

ANCIENT FOREST ™
FRIENDLY

Table of Contents

Foreword

The Laurier Poetry Series began in 2004 with the appearance of *Before the First Word*, a volume of Lorna Crozier's poetry most ably edited by Winnipeg poet Catherine Hunter. Our hope was to bring contemporary Canadian poetry to its readers in a different way—by selecting thirty-five poems from across a poet's career, and by asking the editor and the poet to write an engaging and accessible introduction and afterword, respectively. Crozier and Hunter set the bar very high.

I admit that one ambition I had in mind then—I still do—was to match the reach of the New Canadian Library. I imagined, hoped that what that series has done, mostly for Canadian fiction, the Laurier series would do for Canadian poetry. I hoped that in the high school and university classroom, poets would be better served by a volume that represented their work more widely than the usual anthology, with one or at best a few poems from each poet. And I hoped that more readers, old and new, beyond the classroom, maybe outside of Canada, would find these volumes appealing.

Ten years later, with twenty-five volumes now in print—and with the very recent and happy experience of using ten of the Laurier volumes, including Crozier's, in a fourth-year university class on contemporary Canadian poetry—a warm and vivid image arises in memory of poet Brian Henderson, then as now the Director of Wilfrid Laurier University Press, asking me over a beer on a hot June afternoon in 2002 in Toronto, at the Learneds, whether I might be interested in editing a series like this one. Then as now, I thought the idea was excellent. I didn't know if it would fly, though Brian's was, then as now, an inspired idea. A few more beers and an hour or so later, we agreed to give it a shot.

Over this last (fast!) decade the dedicated group that Brian leads at WLUP—especially managing editor Rob Kohlmeier and his luminous team—have worked with an unimaginably wide range of poets and poetics. To what little I knew in 2004 about publishing, they have added their consummate and patient professionalism.

What continues to inspire me about the Laurier Poetry Series, or LPS, has been its reception across the country. The love and art and passion and intimacy that twenty editors and twenty poets have brought to their volumes;

the innumerable hours and conversations and meetings, the thousands of emails between and among poets and editors and Wilfrid Laurier; the generous reviews in the country's journals; the reception in classrooms and beyond: all of this eloquently speaks to the joyful proliferation of poetry in Canada today—and tomorrow. What a tremendous wealth of poets and readers we have here! What vital riches!

With each new volume, the Laurier Poetry Series hopes to continue to recognize the growing provenance of this wealth, the wide range of these riches. Our poets—and their readers—deserve nothing less.

—*Neil Besner*
General Editor

Biographical Note

An essayist and novelist as well as a poet, Sina Queyras edited an anthology of Canadian poetry published by an American press—*Open Fields: 30 Contemporary Canadian Poets* (2005), from Persea Books. Between 2005 and 2007 she co-curated the path-breaking feminist Belladonna* reading series in New York and was instrumental in bringing Canadian and American poets into conversation. Her website *Lemon Hound* was a crucial literary salon from 2005 to 2015.

She has published five books of poetry. For her third collection, *Lemon Hound* (2006), she received the Pat Lowther Award and a Lambda Literary Award. She served as writer-in-residence at the University of Calgary and there she wrote the bulk of her 2009 collection, *Experessway*. Her most recent book of poetry is *MxT* (2014).

Her novel, *Autobiography of Childhood*, appeared in 2011.

She currently lives and teaches in Montreal.

Of Genre, Gender, and Genealogy: The Poetry of Sina Queyras

Thus far, twenty-first-century poetics has been preoccupied with two ongoing conversations: the perceived divide between lyric and conceptual writing, and the underrepresentation of women and other nondominant subjects.[1] While these two topics may seem epistemologically and ethically separate, they are in fact irrevocably intertwined. Questions of form are, at their root, questions of visibility and recognizability. Will the reader know a poem when she sees it? And will that seeing alter her perception of the world? And how is the form of the poem altered, productively or un-, by the identity politics of its author? Though identity politics are not new, these vital issues have gained new life and new traction in literary spheres. For example, when, in 2012, writer Amy King published *The Count* on *VIDA: Women in Literary Arts*'s website there was a flurry of conversation both on the web and in print regarding women, publishing, and numbers that quantify the data of published authors' genders. Prior to *The Count* American poets Juliana Spahr and Stephanie Young published a controversy-producing piece entitled "Numbers Trouble." In this text Spahr and Young refute claims made by Jennifer Ashton in an article called "Our Bodies, Our Poems" in which Ashton suggests that "by the mid-80s efforts to 'redress the imbalance' had apparently succeeded—women seemed to make up more or less half of the poets published, half the editorial staff of literary magazines, half the faculties of creative writing programs, and so forth" (32). Following Ashton's lead Spahr and Young review women's presence in anthologies and come to resoundingly different conclusions.

In Canada the so-called Numbers Trouble in literary and poetic circles did not get the same kind of attention, at least not immediately. In their introduction to *Prismatic Publics: Innovative Canadian Women's Poetry and Poetics*, editors Heather Milne and Kate Eichhorn cite Young and Spahr's text as one inspiration for their anthology. And at the interstices of issues of genre, gender, and identity is Sina Queyras. Poet, novelist, essayist, critic, blogger, and public intellectual, Sina Queyras has been asking hard questions about the presence of women in intellectual public spaces for years. One of the stunning undercurrents in *Unleashed*, a collection of early blog posts from her influential site *Lemon Hound*, is Queyras's unflinching refrain, "where are the women?" Queyras's poetics pay dogged attention to questions of both representation and genre. In each of the collections of poetry she inhabits tenets of the traditional lyric, while also leveraging the genre open and letting conceptualism in.

Let us start with the lyric. The lyric poem is, at its most traditional a grammatical vehicle that moves the emotions of the speaker from a lost or desired object toward a listener and then out to the reader. The traditional lyric is a three-way intersection held up by "heterosexualized desire" (Homans 570), in which a masculinized "I" speaks "as if overheard" (Duplessis 29) to an equally masculinized "us" and the focus of desire is an absent but desired "she" (Grossman 227). Queyras's lyricism works with these traditional tenets, and troubles them as well. Her lyrics prompt the reader to consider what happens when the traditional structure is rewritten in such a way that there is both repetition of, and connection to, the traditional structure, but also differencing. Queyras's lyric intervenes in the tradition of heterosexualized desire and in so doing brings women into focus.

Queyras's poetics are also conceptual for a number of reasons, though I will focus here on the question of gender. The female subject is of central concern to conceptual writing. Vanessa Place and Robert Fitterman describe conceptual writing as "writing that mediates between the written object (which may or may not be a text) and the meaning of the object by framing the writing as a figural object to be narrated" (15). Unlike the traditional lyric structure, conceptual writing exaggerates the reading process insofar as its "excessive textual properties refuse … the easy consumption of text and the rejection of reading in the larger culture" (Place & Fitterman 25). Queyras's poetics, which are both lyric and conceptual, are quite literally generative. They move across genre lines, create new foci and voices that are often gendered female, and in so doing strengthen poetic genealogies of influence that may otherwise be overlooked.

Queyras is the author of five collections of poetry (*Slip, Teethmarks, Lemon Hound, Expressway, MxT*), one collection of essays (*Unleashed*), a novel (*Autobiography of Childhood*), and scores of born-digital essays of poetic and cultural criticism. She edited *Open Field: 30 Contemporary Canadian Poets*, an American-published anthology of Canadian poets. She is prolific on Twitter, and her single-authored blog *Lemon Hound*, which was established in 2005, has been a multi-authored hub for critical literary and cultural discourse since 2012. Queyras's poetic practice and critical discourse, which take place at the crossroads of the central poetic debates of the twenty-first century, have situated her in a unique position of what the late literary critic Barbara Godard named the ex-centrique. Neither wholly outside nor wholly in, the ex-centrique is an interloper who keeps things current, interesting, and deliberately unsettled. Understand this categorization and Queyras's placement and you will begin to understand central issues of gendered and genre conservatism in twenty-first-century poetry and poetics.

As Canadian critic Lianne Moyes has written, literary history does not quite know what to do with ex-centriques (163). Canonical archiving of Canada's literary production still tends overwhelmingly to be grouped into generic, periodic, or national canons. What role then does the ex-centrique play in constructing a history of literary connections? In some cases, the ex-centrique will play a deceptively stable role. Queyras's poetics can be situated within a Canadian literary history of ex-centriques that has direct connections to the expatriate work of the modernist period. An early attempt to sketch out these contemporary ex-centriques came in 1984 when Godard posited that the creation of a thorough literary history in Canada would require understanding women. Specifically, Godard calls for a rearticulation of literary history that takes into account women's transgressions. She figures Canadian women writers as "ex-centriques," meaning outside the centre. They are also "'telling it slant,' in Emily Dickinson's words," and in so doing "they are transgressing literary codes in a manner approximating madness—hence eccentric" (57). We are back, then, to the subject of women and representation.

Godard suggests that the history of positioning women writers as colonial subjects in relation to patriarchal culture is of especial import when attempting to understand the literary history of Canada. Godard's thesis identifies a "causal link between [women's relationship to established literary discourse] and the pioneering role of women writers in this country, most specifically to the advent of Modernism and Post-Modernism in Canada's literary tradition. The more forcefully they have asserted their feminism, the more disruptive their literary productions have been. Ex-centriques, thus avant garde" (58). In short, Godard proposes a genealogy of women's writing in Canada that is both viscerally connected to oral tradition's marginalized status in the archive, and between Canadian women's literary production in relation to the Modern and Post-Modern periods. Importantly, Godard underscores the problematics of creating this genealogical literary history that is specific to Canada. The problem is that unlike countries where feminist literary and theoretical production has been formative and visible in reacting against the overt exclusion of women from the national canon, in Canada women have been uncannily present. Rather than being a cause for celebration, however, this presence has created a false sense of equality and valuation where there is not one (58). The female subject is abused, lost, replaced. Tracing a contemporary Canadian feminist poetics requires trespassing into genres, regions, and periods that often remain siloed. As I have briefly suggested, posing this question of trespassing in the context of modernist cultural production potentially leads us to the work of "women." As literary historians have argued, the gender of modernism needs not only remediation but also reorientation.

Queyras herself pays little attention to borders and boundaries. Born on the West Coast of Canada, raised in the back of a station wagon criss-crossing the country, a poet, a blogger, an essayist, a teacher, Queyras is an interloper welcome in conversations about conceptual poetry as well as a leader in lyric circles. In *Lemon Hound*, one of the speaker asks, "Who understands trespassing?" The answer, it seems, comes in the poems themselves, which joyfully trespass by crossing genre divides and drawing diverse and enthusiastic inspiration from a radical coterie of literary and artistic influences. Gertrude Stein, Virginia Woolf, Kathy Acker, Vanessa Place. In each of her poetic publications Queyras brings the past and present into collision with a serious and sustained conversation with the future. In other words, Queyras's oeuvre tracks an evolving concern with gender, genre, and the potentially unsustainable future toward which forms and bodies are throttling.

In her first collection, *Slip* (2001), Queyras's poems exhibit the clearest fidelity to the lyric in its traditional Romantic form. A singular speaking subject who reflects on moments of feeling and rupture also navigates the terrain of poetic reflection. However, these reflections occur from the margins of the speaker's own life, and less from moments recollected in tranquility. The opening long poem, "Scrabbling," introduces recurrent themes in Queyras's work. Grief, gender, desire, and literary genealogy rearrange their relatings like so many tiles of the board game. There is, in "Scrabbling," something of the natural world as well. The speaker moves between the relentlessly urban terrain of her new home in "Leonard Cohen's town" to the wildness of her West Coast childhood. The tension between the urban and the wild, between East and West, gets played out as an internal struggle in the speaker herself. What she knows—innate, instinctual—rubs up against the new—concrete, relentless.

Teethmarks (2004) marks a shift in form as well as content. "Me Victorious" exemplifies Queyras's growing experimentation with listing. The poem piles contradictory ways of being a modern subject onto the seemingly singular speaker. Recognition replaces the traditional lyric reflection as the speaker tries on paradoxical identities, practices, and consumer habits. The line, likewise, shifts from verse stanzas to a dense paragraph stating fact after contradictory fact:

me with my full tank of gas and my recycling stacked. Me victorious in red, white, and blue, in clean socks and discount hair; me victorious and tummy full. Me about unconditional market rules. Me about not caring whether our socks are made by infants in Bangladesh, our potatoes sprayed on the outside, or encoded with pesticides in their genes because who has time to worry about that?

The effect is dizzying: the reader comprehends each unit of composition, each subjective utterance, but the form of the poem nips at the heels of the conventional lyric. "TV M/other" exemplifies Queyras's fidelity to her poetic genealogies: the poem reads as both homage and discourse with Anne Carson's TV poems in *Men in the Off Hours* (2000). Here, in Carson's syntactical structure, Queyras probes her own mother's histories and pathologies:

> The women
> > wall to wall
> vacuum,
>
> feather duster
> > rabbit
> tail. You never see
> her (after mid-
> night)
>
> fingers, lips, hair
> loosening, frayed
> at the end,
>
> or longing.

Thus, the lyric subject is doubled and trebled: Carson, the speaker's mother, the speaker.

Lemon Hound (2006) takes formal and genealogical investigations further, pushing again at the boundaries of lyric reflection. Further, using Stein's and Woolf's syntactical experimentation as inspiration, the poems of *Lemon Hound* break language and genre to crack conventional and coercive definitions of gender to their cores. This text also marks Queyras's shifting interest with the tenets of conceptual poetics that encourage process and theoretical investigation as a central part of the poem's construction. Or, in the case of unmaking

Woolf's *The Waves*, deconstruction. Queyras pares down prose to its poetic bones. Gone are the connective tissues of grammar. What remains is not incomprehensible, nor is it unreadable:

> Him Rhoda go under myself how Jinny
> Rhoda go under myself how Jinny Him
> go under myself how Jinny Him Rhoda go
> myself how Jinny Him Rhoda go under
> how Jinny Him Rhoda go under myself
> Jinny Him Rhoda go under myself how

What remains are the spaces between what is knowable and what is claimed to be known.

Expressway (2009), a collection that takes place on, around, and in the architecture of superhighways, plays with limits: the limits of genre, the limits of gender, the limits of so-called progress. In this text lyric subjectivity fractures against the pressures of modernity only to reconstitute itself in the medians of the roadways where the reader is placed among women wielding pickaxes. There is grief for degradation of the environment and of community, but there is also grief at the prospect of giving up hope. "Go forth and undo harm," prescribes the closing proverb. "Go forth and do."

In *MxT* the grief is not only for the lost ones, but also for the historic erasure and rescripting of a poetics of women's affect: from rage to hysteria, women's feelings have been made explainable and thus dismissable. In the waffling—the hesitations—there's the tendency to transcribe that visceral thinking as incoherent, as unsure, as tentative (as though it is a mad characteristic, a characteristic of madness). The poems of this collection mourn lost loved ones, lost literary genealogies, and lost hope. As the speaker swims across oceans of grief she seeks solace in critical theory, in philosophy, in the sacrosanct directness of engineering and circuitry. Yet, here again there is no easy conclusion. No tranquility of reflection soothes the mourner, no amount of time takes away the sting of what has been taken away already. Despair, rage, desire, and longing—the stuff of the traditional lyric—are rerouted through conceptual tactics, visual poems, and insistent reference to other literary ex-centriques.

Moving between the United States and Canada, from page to website, between the Poetry Foundation's blog and her own, Queyras is perhaps a prepositional poet, an ex-centrique whose poetics enact the possibilities of being among more expansive literary genealogies, and re-cite Stein's exploratory syntax. She is a joyful, genre-trespassing poet who is at work inscribing a legacy that "thinks back through mothers," as Woolf encourages. The cover image for this selection, which is a photograph by Queyras herself, is a visualization of that joyful trespassing. Here, the disembodied arm of a plastic doll reaches out to the viewer. Rather than being wholly discomfiting, the synthetic doll's arm is wrapped by a caterpillar acting as a bracelet of sorts. This is a visual poetic that, like Queyras's written work, brings two things together in uneasy, but aesthetic and political connection. Like the barking, living literary *Lemon Hound*, the photograph disrupts expectations and reorients us to new modes of interrelation. Quyeras's citational forms, be they poetic or, in the case of the cover photo, visual, are "disruptive" in Lynette Hunter's sense of the term: Queyras's mothers are queer doers who, through crosstalk and disruption, establish a literary network of ex-centriques that stretches into the twenty-first century.

—*Erin Wunker*

Note

1. See, for example, Goldsmith, Queyras, Place and Fitterman, Milne and Eichhorn, Spahr and Young.

Works Cited

Ashton, Jennifer. "Our Bodies, Our Poems." *American Literary History* 19.1 (Spring 2007): 211–31.

Brydon, Diana, and Marta Dvorak, eds. *Crosstalk: Canadian and Global Imaginaries in Dialogue*. Waterloo: Wilfrid Laurier UP, 2012.

Duplessis, Rachel Blau. "Corpses of Poesy: Modern Poets Consider Some Gender Ideologies of Lyric." *Genders, Races, and Religious Cultures in Modern American Poetry, 1908–1934*. Cambridge: Cambridge UP, 2001. 29–51.

Eichhorn, Kate. "Beyond Stasis: Proceedings of an Unrealized Conference." *Open Letter* Special Issue "Beyond Stasis: Poetics and Feminism Today" 13.9 (Summer 2009): 7–10.

Eichhorn, Kate, and Heather Milne, eds. *Prismatic Publics: Innovative Canadian Women's Poetry and Poetics*. Toronto: Coach House, 2009.

Godard, Barbara. "Ex-centriques, Eccentric, Avant-garde." *A Room of One's Own* 8.4 (Fall 1984): 57–75.

Goldsmith, Kenneth. *Uncreative Writing*. New York: Columbia UP, 2011.

Grossman, Alan. *The Sighted Singer: Two Works on Poetry for Readers and Writers*. Baltimore: Johns Hopkins UP, 1992.

Homans, Margaret. "Syllables of Velvet: Dickinson, Rossetti and the Rhetorics of Sexuality." *Feminist Studies* 2.3 (1985): 569–93.

Hunter, Lynette. *Disunified Aesthetics*. Montreal: McGill-Queen's UP, 2015.

King, Amy. *The Vida Count*. http://www.vidaweb.org/category/the-count/the-2009-count. Accessed January 14, 2016.

Moyes, Lianne. "Discontinuity, Intertextuality, and Literary History: Gail Scott's Reading of Gertrude Stein." In Di Brandt and Barbara Godard, eds., *Wider Boundaries of Daring: The Modernist Impulse in Canadian Women's Poetry.* Waterloo: Wilfrid Laurier UP, 2009. 163–83.

Place, Vanessa, and Robert Fitterman. *Notes Towards Conceptualisms.* Brooklyn, NY: Ugly Duckling Presse, 2009.

Spahr, Juliana, and Stephanie Young. "Numbers Trouble." *Chicago Review* 53.2–3. (Autumn 2007): 88–111.

Queyras, Sina. *Slip.* Montreal: ECW Press, 2001.

———. *Teethmarks.* Roberts Creek, BC: Nightwood Editions, 2004.

———, ed. *Open Field: 30 Contemporary Canadian Poets.* New York: Persea Books, 2005.

———. *Lemon Hound.* Toronto: Coach House, 2006.

———. *Expressway.* Toronto: Coach House, 2009.

———. *Unleashed.* Toronto: Book Thug, 2010.

———. *Autobiography of Childhood.* Toronto: Coach House, 2011.

———. *MxT.* Toronto: Coach House, 2014.

From "Scrabbling"

1.

Apartment-hunting the plateau: dancer, painter, cellist,
two engineers (Good God!), and an over-ripe woman

with pears for teeth who offered a smoke, borrowed a dollar
in return. No decisions yet. One pleasant surprise: Marg's

midnight call. All's well, though TO's all flash and straw,
talk of screenwriting-slash-money, leave poetry behind.

We are neither of us career poets, she says, slipping
your number in. I leave it floating in the still-warm breeze

to let the winds of fate decide. Harmless, harmless, I sing
myself to sleep, and yet I cannot say your name.

2.

Wake to the sun. Chaton mauling a sparrow on the porch
next door where the women fuck so descriptively I want to yell

Doucement, ma clitoris! But where does the accent fall? *La
langue française* eludes me even more than English,

and who can I ask? The women rarely come up for air,
and Sylv crafts harnesses and whips of leather: *I'll fit you*

one! (Mon Dieu.) Who can I tell I've not even seen
the apparatus, never mind one harnessed between my thighs?

Just two days, already my innocence is threatened, my
island fades. Fickle self: apartment-hunting in the plateau,

my heart with L., who knows where my head is, my
body's desire a mystery to me.

5.

And why resolve? In this the autumn of my thirty-first
year, I'm half a continent from home — living single —

for the first, possibly last, time in my life. A student
in Leonard Cohen's town, on stone-laid avenues,

reading poems in cafés and bars: flirt — how could I not?
You talk Toronto for High Holidays. How harmless.

(I'm listening, yes, trying not to imagine you there.)
Finally you lay out the game, an upturned boat,

my nostrils tingling with you, sneezing, you offer
me tissue, offer me coffee, offer me your laugh.

Impossible! How do you know exactly what I lack?
Reach out so easily, so instinctively — the way your elbow

rests in the strut of your flattened hand: your fingertips
undo me.

9.

If I slip now
If my tongue is brash
If my thoughts betray
If my feet numb
If I fall
If my tongue
If the shell cracks
If our knees touch
If words fail
If our eyes meet
If my heart softens
If the sun
If tongue
If word
If numb
If heart skin tongue word embrace

Fall

I will deny it all

From *Jersey Fragments*
"Me Victorious"

Me with my new blue jeans and t-shirt from the Gap; me with pink
underwear and a goldfish shower curtain from Target; me with my
full tank of gas and my recycling stacked. Me victorious in red,
white, and blue, in clean socks and discount hair; me victorious and
tummy full. Me about unconditional market rules. Me about not caring
whether our socks are made by infants in Bangladesh, our potatoes
sprayed on the outside, or encoded with pesticides in their genes,
because who has time to worry about that? Who cares if companies
can own our DNA just as long as we don't have to read that fine print,
and hey, if they're encoding pesticides in DNA, why not antibiotics in
us? Why not Valium or Prozac? And while they're at it, why not do
away with the gene that makes some of us gay, funny, serene, artsy,
bohemian, overly or underly enthusiastic, doubters, promoters, bad
joke-tellers, union sympathizers, shamans, men who clean. Whatever
makes some of us lean the opposite way — whatever opposite is this
week. Just as long as I don't have to think about potatoes in soil: I
prefer to think of french fries all golden and salted, so far removed
from the earth that I believe they are a lab invention, shot out of a
potato gun at one hundred fries per second. I mean I'm okay with
that. I'm okay with unidentifiable transactions, the elimination of
wild unless it's between the sheets and involving me, oh, me oh me
victorious. Me about owning stuff. Me about buying power and
income security. Me victorious over slippages, over fractures of
wonder, over instances of compassion. Me only concerned with
interest rates, credit card limits, cheap flights to hot places where the
sun oh, oh sun oh sun shines twenty-four-seven and water is
chlorinated, contained in cement and plastic, trucked in from places
where other people have to endure rain. Me victorious. Me such a fine
citizen, such a good statistic, such a humble consumer, I vote with my
fashion sense, with my belly, with my God — and he's mine, all mine
only listens to me — turns his back on you, all you, other types. Me, oh,

me victorious with my credit card, with my well-heeled acceptance, with my condoning and tolerance, my blind eyes, my skill at skirting you on the street, my ability to step over, to go around, to sink lower, my cavernous depths of denial. Me victorious over sleepless nights. Over worrying. Me Nyquil, me Sleep Ease, me Johnny Walker, me Budweiser, me Imitrix, me a totally hot babe. Me laser aerobics, me a new Volkswagen Golf, me Googling, me Googled, me full of the best intentions, me a suicide bomber with a long, slow burn, me just want the Dream, me want the lottery, me want that change, me just want to believe the only thing holding anyone back is their own lack of hard work.

From *Dizzy, or, My Mother's Life as Cindy Sherman*
"TV M/other"

She watches her m/
other
self   round in a
black and white
Remember
          channels?

          Correction,
She does not watch
herself,
          turns
(Look it's on!)
          when she
is on: aproned
smiling, grocery list
mind.

The gaps are not:
          visible
(of course)   or squint.
It could be comical.
When the camera
pans to his stubble
and pec

          the women
                    wall to wall
vacuum,

feather duster
          rabbit
tail. You never see
her (after mid-
night)

fingers, lips, hair
loosening, frayed
at the end,

or longing.

> Dead babies
line the cellar
stairs

Come.

(oh come, come on)

"Roadside Memory #1"

Five kids and
pee
construction. Cars crawling
     beetles on
sweltering
and muffled
      mops her breasts, tulip
and ochre shift, floral, sweat (her waist,
he can put his hands around her wait).

She points   neon
     a lighthouse, but he will not
never will do what she wants,
needs
     crying
she throws herself out
of the moving Valiant (black
red interior, red beaks) and walks:
it is Calgary. 1959. A man at a desk
lurid, puce (she understands this now) face
pockmarked but still, manners: May I?
     she feels the sweat
in her brassiere, imagines a swimming pool
the sound of slot machines, nickel and dime
(Oh God, the heat)
in the hall. Lack of air
(someone has leaned on the prairie,
elbow of shale, thumb of treeline)
     almost turning back, hoping
      at the side of the road,
       impatience. Angry. Controlling. Door
corrugated   small, knob
     and foul. Shaving mirror, light bulb, window
(Who brought the f'ing cat? Who lost the house? Who could not
pay the bills?) and someone knocking.

This is private,
her dress. She hovers, trembling
          a lady never sits
(she is faint now) and suddenly banging
in here, she says again,   face seeping,
scurry of   in the sink
          here, she says, again,   harder, now
          she sways
pees on her shoes, reaching
to the sink for balance, pulls
now scrambles, yelling
pounding. She opens the window
as far as she can and cat-thin
          midsection of
hip bones bruised
she stands on the sink, snaps her
hips, hinges through
dirty laundry, head
first into
clatter of garbage

From *A river by the moment*
"The river is all thumbs"

She is feeling brisk at the heel. She loves feeling brisk at the heel. She is feeling brisk at the heel and rivering her thumbs. She is at the edge of cool. She runs her thumbs along the hinge of river. She loves running her thumbs along the hinge of river. She feels river. She feels thumb. She is brisk and thumbing. She is numb and loving. She is feeling loving. She is feeling loving about feeling. She loves feeling about loving. She loves feeling about feeling. She loves feeling about feeling loving. Her loving feels. Her loving loves rivers. She is feeling loving about rivers. She loves feeling loving about rivers. She is feeling rivers about loving feeling. She rivers about loving. She rivers about feeling. She rivers about the hinges of rivers. Her feelings hinge. She hinges about feelings. She hinges about feeling the river of hinges. She is feeling thumbs. She loves feeling about her thumbs. She is feeling about her thumbs as she rivers her feelings. Her thumbs river. Her feelings cool. She feels cool rivering her thumbs. She feels her thumbs hinge the river and cooling she thumbs. She loves feeling that her thumbs hinge the river. She thumbs numb love.

"Whose genealogy?"

To claim genealogy, to bear the burden of, to be
stepped on, dug up and dumped in, to be pissed on,
built on the back of, scaled with brick, wood, to be
lashed with rubber, tarred, to have your shale ribs
cracked; to be sold, developed, shaped and reshaped
by individuals, groups, soldiers, with witnesses,
within earshot, under open windows, in your father's
house; is to be exploded, chemicalled, dredged,
mined, bombed, sheared, made a monument of; is to
be tethered and tamed, mapped, photographed,
marveled at, shit on; is to be mowed, moved, moni-
tored, circled, scoured; is to be made over, to be seen
as passive, always, to bear the burden of resistance
and maintenance, beginning and end, all in the
folds of; to believe in special relationships: one
breast of all breasts; to mourn the drying up of milk, the
tumorousness of nurture, the arms that surround
nothing, the zero of once was, gone, past tense, now
undeniably something else.

"If only"

If only men were more feminine. If only Judaism were more feminine. If only industry were more feminine. If only bridges were more feminine. If only trucks were more feminine. If only airplanes were more feminine. If only fruit were more feminine. If only engines were more feminine. If only economics were more feminine. If only test tubes were more feminine. If only physicists were more feminine. If only space were more feminine. If only Hollywood were more feminine. If only America were more feminine. If only farmyards were more feminine. If only the weather were more feminine. If only Islam were more feminine. If only engineers were more feminine. If only city planners were more feminine. If only feminists were more feminine. If only Catholicism were more feminine. If only politicians were more feminine. If only astronauts were more feminine. If only corporations were more feminine. If only women were more feminine. If only what was feminine were firm. If only there were slots. If only things fit inside.

"I?"

If you open your mouth, ache. If you don't open your mouth, swelter. If you open your mouth but hold your breath, ether. If you look for colour, coral and tea leaves. If you follow the moon, wet and concrete. If you cling to the earth, pistol and candy apple. If You give up your garden, maze and globe, hydrangeas and moon vines. If you lose your shoes, pumice and strain. If you have no money, tin, linen, clang. If you lie down with dogs, pale and tender. If you watch television, carrot and yanking. If you embrace nothing, luster and tar. If you know sorrow, whistle and salt. If you lie down with birds, currents and vertigo. If you breathe, corpuscular and crepuscule. If you can, software and lingerie. Is you should, totem, forelock, tibia, stamen. If you are blonde, topple, flax, moraine. If you love flowers, do not fold. If you follow the sun, straw and oval. If you hide, velvet and myrrh. If you are a redhead, pepper and artichoke. If you eat only limes, Knossos and paddle. If you sing, ozone, crackle and stir. If you are wanting, scathed and shrouded. If you open your eye, salt lick and clover. If you lie down with cats, ankle and dock. If you follow your heart, sledgehammer. If you embrace all, oarlock and tidal. If you look for light, spleen, splint. If you follow the earth, spade and compass. If you lie down with fish, ice cube and convection. If you know anger, detonate and flex. If you give up walls, columbine and feather. If you are still here, present and peel, dandelion and lemon hound.

From *On the scent*

"1."

Here she is inside. Walls and windows. Appendages and openings. Here she is sitting on a stack of books. Here she is digging out from under an avalanche of paper. Here she is swatting words with her coattails. Here she is wondering what to do with outdated memory. Here she is boxing and unboxing. Here she is moving stuff. Here she is deleting whole files, randomly. Here she is perplexed at the mounds of paper. Here, I tell you, here she is hiding under the Xerox machine. Here she is communing with resonators. Here she is clucking the MRI tune. Here she is earplugged and eyeshadowed. Here she is tall and long in the stride, here she is a force of circulation. Here she is sideways in a windstorm. Here she is teal and persimmon. Here she is Italian plum. Here she is the palest interior of a pomegranate. Here she is. Here she is in Banana Republic. Here she is black and black. Here she is thinking of the colour blue. Here she is trying to see underwater. Here she is reading on the train to New York. Here she is wiping coffee from the seat. Here she is sitting next to seven young rappers, pants like circus tents, du-rags and ball caps piled on high. Here she is. Here she is in an office in Philadelphia thinking of the letter R. Where would we be without R, she asks? Where would we be without E? Where would we be without arms? Here she is with meringue and milquetoast. Here she is hiding behind a maple tree in October, the weather having changed too quickly and she without a sweater. Here she is walking down Bleecker thinking, how? How? How can she describe

the windmill of her aorta? How tibia is her confu-
sion? How like the Microsoft song her frustration
flits and crescendos. How like the blue of the xp
screen her mood flickers in the traffic-jam hour. How
archaic the need to open a window and breathe.

"4."

The women plug themselves in. They work hard.
They untwist bread bags and dole out dabs of butter.
They choose low-fat milk. They have bought digital
cameras. They join food co-ops. They find recycling
sources. They mail things diligently. They see the
sun as unlimited potential. Aureole and blister,
thumbs and jelly, websites and manifestos. The
women are red. They are preoccupied with shows.
They subscribe to green. Thoughts extend like awn-
ings. Inscription and tongue, wireless cards and
upgrades, the women circulate petitions. They for-
ward articles about Björk and Rachel Corrie. They
organize demonstrations, worry over hoarfrost on
lemon groves. They delegate. They multi-task. The
women press their foreheads against granite.

The women are blue. They consider heels an option.
They have unplugged Ani and plugged in Radio-
head. They are amused. They toast veggie dogs and
buy organic; some of them embrace beef. They wear
Birkenstocks, they smoke cigars, they wear their hair
long or they shave it. They find time. They buy soy.
They surf. They bookmark Bitch, Slut, Whore. They
are sworn to transgress. They diss meatloaf and
socks with sandals. They buy appliances. Everyone is
witty. They blend fabrics. They make their own porn.
They know the eighteenth century.

The women are burgundy. They discover obscure
cases of women. They take notes. They take classes.
They discover points of departure. They cut a wide
swath. They dream of seducing Björk. They are not
tongue-tied. They are not fooled by nature. They
create gardens of air, orchid and oxalis. Some have

discovered Lucinda Williams. They read Stein. They are not good girls. Some women are prismatic. Everyone is just liberal enough. The women often unplug themselves. They penetrate. They let their hair grow. They find a good masseuse. They have never read Mary Daly. They go shopping for shoes. They are divided by shoes. They cannot get over shoes. The shoes corral them. The groups divide further.

The women are pink. They shop for appliances. They fix cars and join car clubs. The women wave at each other across the gaps. They are always running out of batteries. The women strut and feather themselves. They buy hair products. They buy eye cream even if they love wrinkles. They have all read *The Handmaid's Tale* and tucked it away neatly. Despite everything, race continues to divide. The women are plugged in. The women carry their laptops into gardens. The women embrace only so much integration. Some women are salmon. Some women have turned in their diamonds for pens. The women have credit cards. They are relieved feminism is over. They are proud of their humour. They don't wear tampons lightly. They blend colours. They feel bad about Martha Stewart. They have given up on Madonna. They meditate. They read. They don't do the right thing. They make gardens in matchboxes.

Miracles of green, they are mechanical. They find ways to breed with women. They start businesses, they discuss tax rates, pass on words of advice. They cajole and banter. They have potlucks. They are all disappointed with Hillary. They have barn raisings; no roof is too high, or too wide. Beam and lathe; hammer and throng. They masturbate and seduce. They have appliances and they know how to use them. They wear spaghetti straps and heels. They wear overalls and boots. They spit. They gesticulate. Their hair is shale and limestone. They attend lesbian baby showers. Civil and chardonnay: unbelievable cunning. They worry about footwear. They get excited about leather. They remember Barbie. They work out. They run. They do seven kinds of yoga. They buy magazines and try new diets. They consider law school. They are not afraid of engineering. They are great shoppers. They demand value.

The women are red. The women are full of themselves. The women kibbutz and spritz. They spin discs. They worry about piercing. They buy books online. They regret there is no more need for women-only spaces. They remember women's bookstores with only a tinge of regret. They are full bodied, they are sweltering, they are rock and graphite, purloined and vegan, heavy hipped and encyclopedic. They are annotated. They invite the optic. They embrace titanium. They shed their skin daily. Others gather it. There are bags of us in a basement. Earth is there too, aluminum, and feather.

"5."

The mothers were feminists. The mothers marched.
The mothers wore purple and read Betty Friedan.
The mothers listened to Janis Ian and Ferron. The
mothers dropped out. The others went to Michi-
gan and danced topless. The mothers used menstru-
ation cups. The mothers tie-dyed everything and
cooked meals from *Moosewood*. The mothers had
committee meetings. The mothers subscribed to *Ms.*
and believed in affirmative action. The mothers wore
Birkenstocks and dreamed of living in Vermont or
Saltspring. The mothers ate dried fruit and brown
rice. The mothers lived in the suburbs and shopped.
They fought to build credit ratings. The mothers
wore sweater sets. The mothers knew nothing of
feminism. The mothers ran off to Los Angeles. The
mothers liked to sunbathe. The mothers discovered
Paxil and Prozac. The mothers went to Holt's; they
discussed Bloomingdale's and Saks. The mothers
listened to Neil Diamond and sewed skirts. The
mothers had sharp tongues. The mothers went to
the opera. The mothers had good educations. The
mothers had nothing to say. The mothers voted for
Reagan or Mulroney. The mothers read *Newsweek*
and *Cosmo*. The mothers read Alice Walker. The
mothers held down two jobs, raised children and
continued to believe. The mothers moved forward,
hesitant, never sure what they had won, or what was
merely yet to be revealed.

From *Virginia, Vanessa, the strands*
"There was the moment of the puddle in the path"

And the puddle was the word. And the puddle reflected everything. And the puddle grew. And the puddle spoke back. And the puddle was nothing. The puddle unplugged her. It drained her. And the puddle was silent. The puddle went on forever, it struck fear in her. And the puddle was thin and spreading. The puddle spoke Greek and the puddle knew all. The puddle wore britches. It knew precisely what she was thinking. And the puddle sunk deeper. And the puddle haunted. And the puddle grew before her. And the puddle divined the word. And the puddle engulfed her. And the puddle made her still. And the puddle made her grow tall. And the puddle froze her. The puddle scorned. It laughed. The puddle meant business. The puddle threatened. The puddle reached out. The puddle snatched at her ankles. The puddle was monstrous. The puddle had hands. The puddle was mundane. The puddle smelled of spring. The puddle contained five volumes of the lives of the poets; it carried paper sailboats. The puddle was a birdbath. The puddle was filled with tadpoles. The puddle went on forever. The puddle was bottomless; it contained the cosmos. The puddle smelled like cocoa. Beetles swam in it. Cotton wool gathered. Ants bathed. The puddle was dirty. The puddle reflected everything. The puddle embraced her. The puddle saw up her skirt. The puddle shamed her. The puddle was a mirror. The puddle shattered her. The puddle was larger than life. The puddle was irreverent. The puddle needed to be put in its place.

From *Meanwhile, elsewhere, otherwise*
"Some other poets and the puddle"

> 'When for no reason I could discover, every-
> thing suddenly became unreal.'
>
> Virginia Woolf

She didn't notice the puddle. She was busy unravel-
ling the pavement. She clip-clopped past. She had
serious business. The words in her head were pleas-
ing her. She liked the sun. The smell of meat sizzling
called out to her. Language needed to be parted,
ordered. The children irritated her as they played in the
puddle. They were noisy. It was not her business.
There were no books in the playground, but there
were shapes to things. Sentences combusted. No
one recognizes. The words in her head grew cold.
They needed a rest. Her feet had an idea. She
thought they meant business. She saw herself in
everything and everything was good.

She saw the puddle as pewter. She swallowed it sweet
as figs. She saw it nestled in the cleavage of plum
girls. She held them over her head and cracked their
legs.

She saw the universe in the puddle. She saw a slide
show of organic compounds. She saw the key and
the key fit. She saw the genital-less amoeba as a
hero. She put her ear to the puddle but she was no
naïve child; she was listening for the rumble of
trucks, not the sweet musings of water beetles.

She waited until winter and when the puddle froze
over, she glided across it. She sat in the summer heat

and was content. She lifted the puddle and slid it down her arm like a pancake. She invited a girl gang over and drank it. She had no puddles on her street. She had no street. She leapt over the puddle on horseback in pursuit. She saw streams of Nazis skimming boot black across the surface. She thought she heard the apostles and so kneeled down to pee. She dove in, scraping her nose. She had her father drain all the puddles in the village. She splashed. She leapt and bombed it with rocks. She floated and toppled heads of Barbie dolls. She walked around. Then she walked around again. She heard men flinging mud and arranged a blanket of oak leaves across the surface. She did a cartwheel. She knit a scarf out of the letters R and E which she wound round and round and round.

From The Waves, *an unmaking*
"...*The Waves*, an architecture"

Him Rhoda go under myself how Jinny
Rhoda go under myself how Jinny Him
go under myself how Jinny Him Rhoda
under myself how Jinny Him Rhoda go
myself how Jinny Him Rhoda go under
how Jinny Him Rhoda go under myself
Jinny Him Rhoda go under myself how

is my with that on are the
my with that on are the is
with that on are the is my
that on are the is my with
on are the is my with that
are the is my with that on
the is my with that on are

the and I of a to in
and I of a to in the
I of a to in the and
of a to in the and I
a to in the and I of
to in the and I of a
in the and I of a to

some our up out her us which
our up out her us which some
up out her us which some our
out her us which some our up
her us which some our up out
us which some our up out her
which some our up out her us

it as not we me have at
as not we me have at it
not we me have at it as
we me have at it as not
me have at it as not we
have at it as not we me
at it not we me have at

...

one like this am for be said
like this am for be said one
this am for be said one like
am for be said one like this
for be said one like this am
be said one like this am for
said one like this am for be

...

...

From *The Endless Path of the New*
"A Memorable Fancy"

At the toll booth she stopped to ask who was in charge of the expressway, or future, the words slipping back and forth in front of her. A large-headed woman, her hair roped and lashed about her head, looked up and held out her hand: *George Washington. Seven times.*

I have no money, she said, suddenly aware this was indeed a fact, as was the yoke around the woman's upright neck. Her nostrils flared, her body strained against it, Al Green in the background. *Are you a poet?* she asked, meaning do you feel that tug? *The roar of the tires is the rhythm of my day,* the woman said, *every fourteen cars a sonnet.* Behind her the city slickened: vehicles everywhere, idling, honking, revving, stiffening themselves against her. The braided woman did not flinch. *George Washington, seven times*

I am lost, she said. *Can you tell me where to start?*

The braided woman's thumbs smoother the air. *You can try Port Authority. But I wouldn't hold my breath.*

In response to the woman's kindness, she shared her latest vision: Louis XVI is alive and living in Washington, a staggeringly blind man filling his frame with BBQ ribs and glazed ham. Under his bed he keeps a rifle, thinking a cattle rustler might show up in the night. Deeply suspicious of his dreams he hires a young woman to stand in the corner and lash herself all night as he sleeps.

It doesn't matter if I see her, he said, *it's knowing she is somewhere lashing herself.*

From *Some Moments from a Land Before the Expressway*
"Lines Written Many Miles from Grasmere"

Grasmere, May – December 1800

1

Wm and John set off into Yorkshire
Cold pork in their pockets.
I could hardly speak when I gave

Wm a farewell kiss. Walked

As long as I could amongst the stones,
Wood rich, palish thick, and resolved
To write a journal of the time till

Wm and J. return. My resolve shall

Give Wm pleasure when he comes …
That I had a letter from Wm! Came on
Just when I was going, went forward

Much amused by stepping-stones.

Sauntered a little
Melancholy in my
Back.

4

To lakeside in the morning
To the waterfall
On the hill above the house,

gathered wild Thyme with my 'load.'

Again upon the hill, more plants
To the Blind man's
As far as the Blacksmith's

By Loughrigg
No Wm!
I slackened my pace.

14

Sunshiny coldish hackberry crab
Blossom, anemone nemorosa, marsh
Marigold speedwell, beautiful blue

Butterflies and Wm asleep

In the window, his chest, the hills hoary,
A winter look; God stripping the trees,
Forms I skimmed, what freedom storms.

Wm haunted with altering the Rainbow.

Swallows come to the sitting-room
Twitter and bustle, hang, bellies
To the glass, forked fish-like tails

Swim round

And round again they come,
Wm (again) attempting to alter,
The added a little Ode.

From *The Endless Hum*
"Murmurings, Movements or Fringe Manifesto"

O little expressway, miracle of expressway, upended galaxy,
extended Adirondack slither, downhill from Syracuse to
Manhattan, glorious, glorious, no longer carrying but being
us, us moving everywhere, all around the globe.

She asserts herself into the grain:
B: Writing is not a commodity.
A: (Unless published).
B: Original is not a commodity
A: (Unless patented).
B: Writing is thinking made visible
A: (Unless it isn't).
B: Original is what you haven't seen
A: (What hasn't been reproduced).
B: Writing is a disordered hum
A: (What is disordered is useless to the market).
B: Original is singing
A: (Recognizable).
B: Writing is always forward
A: ( ).
B: Original is what you don't recognize
A: (What you don't recognize isn't there).
B: Writing is the space between this
A: (Original is overrated)
B: And this
A: (Is anomaly)
B: Space
A: (Who needs this?)
B: Is only in relation to stopping whereas
   Language
A: (Only what is functioning)

B: Persists and
   Original is ornery
A: (Of no value on its own).
B: Or, if somewhere in the suburbs?
A: ( )
B: This dynamite stinks of poem.
A: One morning thousands showed up and inch
   By inch tore up the expressway and carried it off in their beaks.
B: In another city they tore their earmuffs, unplugged
   The white-noise machines, hung up their car keys,
   And took to the pavement in wonder.
   In another city, frozen citizens dropped to their bellies
   Like penguins sliding toward the Great Lakes.
A: The expressway is the future.
   The expressway is the market.
   The expressway is the line endless.
   The expressway contains multitudes.
   The expressway directs and projects.
   The expressway with its chapel and truck stops,
B: Its whorehouses and science centres,
   Its indiscriminate will to connect.
A: They are outside, moving things.
B: Under the sun, moving things.
A: On the horizon, moving things.
B: This one sweeping.
A: All across the land, men out on back steps looking.
B: When a man looks what does he see?
   When a man with his hardhat, when a man in boots.
   When a man reaches out his hand.
   When a man becomes a man.
A: When a woman becomes a man.
   When a woman looks at a man.
   When a woman in her hardhat, when a woman in boots.
   When a man sees a woman.
B: When the woman is not young.

A: is not yet old.

B: When the day is long.

A: is cool and longing.

B: When the woman is nowhere to be found.
   When the man with his stop sign.

A: When the cars, all of them surround us.

B: ( )

A: Thinking is not hostile.

B: She insists against the grain.

A: One or more of you will die. One in four, seven in ten,
   nine in ten, one in twenty, twelve in eighteen, fifty-fifty or
   roll the dice, luck of the draw, dice of the throw, tip of the
   cup, turn of the wheel, toll of the table, ace of spade,
   shovel of hearts, dig of luck, stroke of break, deuces wild,
   obtuse, obdurate, crazy as cousins, a statistic in kind, a
   hovering in lamb.

A & B: The poem refuses to start from a position of safety and
   end in a position of safety having momentarily revealed
   a tiny fracture in human existence, the equivalent of a fly
   (a very small one, possibly a fruit fly even) in the chardon-
   nay, or perhaps even more revelatory, a does of chemo-
   therapy (but not yours), a glimpse into the abyss (a tiny
   one, twice removed) and back to the front porch (this
   could be yours), before the next sip, because the poem is
   a connector, the poem is not a country lane, there is
   nowhere that doesn't lead here, there is nowhere here
   cannot find there. Everywhere is capable of being here
   now. There is nowhere this is not. There is nowhere I.

Proverbs of Hell

The body sublime, the heart suv.
Fuel your plow with the blood of war.
Drive your car on the bones of the dead.
The road of co_2s leads to rising seas.
He who is preoccupied with the afterlife pisses on the present.
So the price of oil goes, so goes the number of wars.
A fool sees product; a wise man sees shade.
He who sullies the earth sullies himself; he who dulls the sun
    dulls his senses.
The future is the reversal of destruction.
Even a bee's too busy.
Profits are measured by the dollar, but real profit cannot be
    measured.
A wholesome food comes in fewer than sixteen pieces from
    seven states.

Prisons are built with the bricks of luxury items.

Let man wear the fell of the hemp seed, woman the fleece of
    cotton.
The bird a thought, the spider a path, the mind the means.

What was once proved and known is now only rarely imagined.
What was once used to imagine now operates software.
The rat, the mouse, the starling, the squirrel; the lion, the
    tyger, the elephant, the whale – only the useless, or root-
    less, survive, otherwise: extinction porn.
The cistern pollutes; the fountain overflows, is of no use to
    itself.
Once thought filled immensity; now it purchases goods.
To speak your mind is to be unpatriotic; to be human, then,
    is to be unpatriotic.
All things imagined must be images of truth; all things
    created must be fragments of our imagination.

The eagle never wreaked so much havoc as when he
     submitted to the whims of profit.
The eagle provides for himself, but the air provides for the
     eagle.
Want in the morning. Buy at noon. Buy in the evening. Buy
     in your sleep.
He who has suffered you to impose on him knows the market.
As the plow follows the markets, so the market follows itself.
The tygers of the market are no wilier than the corporate dogs.
Expect poison form the standing mind.
The coals of Wall Street, the bricks of despair, the last drop,
     the last grain.
As the cat chooses the warmest place to curl her bones so the
     wise man seeks home.
To create a new kind of flower is the splice of genes.
The best wine is the oldest, the best thought is the first.
Cheerfulness is the hammer of the right.

The expressway is a straight line, but the crooked road
     remains the road of genius.

Where man is, nature is bereft.
Where nature is not man, is not known.
Where nature is not natural, man is not man.

As a dog returns to his vomit, so a citizen to his belief in
     separation.
More is destruction.
Less is the wisdom of the future.
Abundance is all context.
The end of thought is the end of man is the end of earth.
In abstentia, in absence, in obsolesce, or obnoxious.
Where nature is, man is not enough.
Enough, or too much. Too much.

Go forth and undo harm.

Go forth and do.

ALTERNATING
MOURNING

With Alternate Mourning (AM), grief flows in both directions and may completely reverse itself. Far from being an unstable conduit for grief, AM allows for greater depth of feeling to flow more efficiently over greater distances. The downside to more deeply felt grief is a need for insulation to step down emotions for common transmission. Consumer mourning outlets vary according to countries, size of populations and equipment. The horizontal axis measures time, the vertical axis measures grief.

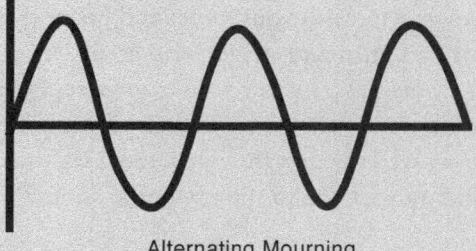

Alternating Mourning

"Water, Water Everywhere"

'I see' 'with my voice.' – Alice Notely, *The Descent of Alette*

Water, water everywhere, my dead ones, and you wading through ferns to my window, a cat on a buoy, a rabbit on a paddle, a dog with a bowl in her mouth, water rising, water advancing and yes, yes, that is me, swimming through milk of the sky, not a speck of barnacle underfoot.

Water, water, everywhere, bodies, gliding, feathered, furred, sweet pink and brown, your skins, you come to me with your blue eyes and your brown eyes, with your violet and green eyes, you come into my arms that hush and stride, Mother, Father, your legs that kick and strut, my pets, I carry you in my sleep, you come and I have saved my tuna water, I have made a meal of egg and rice for you, I have saved my best thoughts, too, I lay them at the foot of the bed and wait for you to slip under the door.

Water, my dead ones, and you with your ravaged look. It sometimes takes hours for you to face me, other times you have brought your own utensils, you come and I am open, you swim through my ribs.

My love, to love is to lose your love, to lose; the hand is emptied, if I turn away, if the rain stops, if I am silent … all the formulas for turning back time.

.

Grief is a century of death, and a century of death before that, and before that, I want to bring you into the fold, Death, I want to drag you right into the mall, the earth, which is made of death.

I think about Thích Nhất Hạnh smiling every time someone puts her foot on the brake. I see the smiling Buddah in the brake lights too, but more importantly I wonder how he drives in those long robes and then I think of course he doesn't drive, and it's easier to find the brake lights amusing.

I found the brake lights of the car I rear-ended last month alarming. I was calling out to you, my dead ones, I was calling you home, and I smashed into something solid and I forgot about breath.

.

I want to love my memory of you, it's not a conceptual feeling though I can attempt a grid of my feelings for you, I can calculate the number of verbs, and adverbs; I can leave a how-to diagram on the coffee table if you would like to look at it when I finally sleep.

.

I am feeling about you the way waves feel about the shore. You come at me in endless loops, your moods, the looks on your faces, my lost ones, more alive by the minute, and the colour in your faces tinting with the seasons.

.

I am not interested in what Bourdieu, or Kristeva, has to say about grief. I don't want a grid. I want arms. I don't want a theory; I want the poem inside me. I want the poem to unfurl like a thousand monks chanting inside me. I want the poem to skewer me, to catapult me into the clouds. I want to sink into the rhythm of your weeping, I want to say, *My grief is turning and I have no way to remain still.*

I am not interested in feeling by proxy; I go to the hollow when I want to empty, I go to theory when I want to sit with someone else's thinking, I go to myself when I want to see you.

I am feeling about clover, I inhale and it honeys my lungs: if I finally do catch you and put my mouth to yours you will taste that summer.

When I am being torn apart, I don't need you to point out the empty seed pods of winter.

You won't find a couplet in the wild, my love; a sestina is a formal garden, a villanelle is the court, a sonnet is an urban love story, an epic is the senate, a prose poem is the city.

I am not interested in other words for honey. I am interested in honey.

I saw Mary Oliver on Cypress. The rough angles of the coastal mountains terrified her. Later she appeared on Spanish Banks looking west. *Distance is helpful,* she said, *but size isn't: this is too raw for poetry.* I dropped her in Stanley Park, I thought she might be more comfortable wandering the groomed paths.

I am operating on instinct here, the way the guy at the beach chooses his rocks to stack and the rocks never topple, they are grey on grey against grey, modular bodies, sturdy, flat, fat as islands.

I can't be worried about offending Mary. I can't weigh my grief against a pound of flesh. I have a right to order the driftwood or not. Whole nations have been built on description.

Mourning, like a thigh appearing in the blue light of winter.

.

Choose your memories well, my love, death is a long meditation.

.

Wanting is exhausting; in death have we let yearning go?

.

I read Mary Oliver's poem about angels dancing on the tip of a pin and I kept thinking, *She is writing about a penis, Mary Oliver is really a gay man and everything is about* AIDS, which made me want to carry Mary Oliver in my pocket.

.

How many shapes will you visit me in, Death? How many gestures – each a stitch in the belly. The entire woodland echoes with your filthy mouth, the neon tree, the leaf flickering a sequin in green velour, my flickering rock, my soft bowl, my leafy gasket, you bring me thoughts of the purest vials of amphetamine. You burn like the skin of a spider, laugh with the bounce of a rabbit, and yes, I do remember Spanish Banks, the city diorama in Le Creuset, and later, burning your prescriptions in a cucumber mist, that heron appearing suddenly, so casual in his faded Chelsea coat, his prehistoric beak and yellow eye watching as I burned enough OxyContin to tile a small bathroom.

.

Sappho says in the house of song there shall be no mourning, but all song is mourning. All shapes reflect absence; I have collected all the bits of soap, every trace that can still float, and strung them from the rafters.

I am here with my flesh and my thoughts, trying to let go of you.

I see you in Carolee Schneeman, banging the floor with a broom. I see you in the black, stacked shapes of Louise Nevelson, I see you in Andrea Zittel's *Escape Vehicle*, we are floating form island to island. I see you in Metro Pictures, there are endless reels of you moving stones from one side of a field to another. Who would you have been had you understood realism? Blood pooling in fur cups, boardrooms filled with hundreds of babies? A screen the shape of a jellyfish floating through a park? You can give a girl a cleaver but you can't make her swing.

Under all that rage, joy, big as the pills in Damien Hirst's mirrored cabinet, a caplet so huge you could parasail across the bay.

Good attracts good and so on.

The emergency of women is the emergency of the world. We say, *What good is history if we have not felt it?* We say, *Don't let the dead go until you have tasted them.*

How does one see? A thing in movement, a pail attached to a tall spiky wood, snow, spring, light? What is the beetle carrying? How banana a slug? What temperature mist? How glisten the leaf tremble?

Judith Butler at Princeton on the ethics of violence. The 'I' cannot tell the story of how it came to be – we may only become self-knowing by engaging in non-judgment. The self that propels the narrative is no longer, but the narrative goes on.

Who is that narrative?

Who is I?

Who is happy?

Who is singing? Who are we singing to? Ruth? Shulamith?
Solomon? Son of Samuel? Buddha? Mother? Is it the man with
no hands on the subway floor? Is it the last iceberg? Is it Dada? Is
it you, my love?

Fuck you, you say, *fuck art, fuck cancer, fuck your empty gestures,
fuck every way we are contained, every way we are numbed, fuck
your female heroes with their trembling lips and short tethers.*

*Fuck the way you see me as a fence post, fuck fence posts. Fuck the
way you rely on women's work. Fuck the way you absent us from
your conversations. Fuck Bellow, fuck Olson, fuck Berryman, fuck
rhetoric, fuck you.*

Take this anger; wipe your face with it, take your career and
douse it in kerosene, walk away from it, you do not do, you do
not do, grief, in your pointed shoes.

Everything has been critiqued, everything has been pho-
tographed, Diane Arbus took advantage of the freaks, Lee Miller
finally turned the tables on the gaze, but she photographed more
death than she made surreal masterpieces.

My love for you floats across architecture, lets the wind lift its
skirt, refuses to be tamped down.

I am not angry – what smart person wouldn't want to fuck art? Or fuck in art? Or be fucked by art, her clean lines so hard and bright?

I call you from Matthew Marks, from Gagosian, tracing the lines of a huge Richard Serra curve. I have seen so much thinking gleaming, I want to roll it too, make it big, manly, I want to ride it through Manhattan, but mostly I want it solid, a deep root tethering me, an unflappable sense of calm. Are you calm now? I see you in the Arbus retrospective, furtive glances at the journals, you want to be angry but you can't stop looking and when you look you love and when you love the entire world un-folds around you, you are so bright you make the security guards flinch, lurch, pat the mics on their chests.

The future at a hundred miles an hour, mouths stretched like windsocks. I hate your seamless layers, you know that, but you scratch by, and I am thinking of all the Trojan horses this bay has seen, eleven of them now, bobbing in the harbour, containing who knows what army of product.

Unbelievable views, never did take them for granted. There is a spot just outside the pillar and glass where, when you stand in the pea gravel and whisper to me, standing where I am standing by the totem at the edge of the continent, we can hear all the dead ones singing.

"Dear One"

Dear One, the future has crumbling infrastructure and more rain than ice, but there we are, peeking out like the tiny flowers that appear in the cracks under sills. Dear One, I am struggling to be in my body, struggling to stay where I am; I want to be closer to my memory of you. I am adrift without it.

Here in this city that does not love me, the sky falls like sheets of concrete, my days are a loud vertical assembly line of grey, crowding out the loops of pinks and purples, but no longer joy. The gentle men of my gym line up at the window on Papineau, shins in hand, heads turned momentarily away from the hockey game to the trees still trembling from autumn's threading.

Dear One, I can't shake you. It's my fault I am unhappy here. I am the only tree on the block refusing to let my leaves fall. I ride the light; I ride the future thinking of crinoline and cold white wine.

"Like a Jet"

> Little streams passed all over their bodies.
>> Walt Whitman, *Leaves of Grass*

1

A hole in the sky where softness hung.
A crater where the world was, a moment
The size of Manhattan: amazed
We are not all sliding in.

I skirt abjection, drag my nails against
The hours. My eyes for one more glimpse,
Ochre (August, the rough tear of cotton,
The lace and wire, a harness of

Clinging). There is no shrugging off
Weight, no exit ramp, no ease or release,
Perpetual shoulders on orange alert, jaw
Scraping the floor, the body contorts,

The body is fluid: I am leaking,
I no longer care who sees me leak.

2

I held her briefly at the end because finally
She could not scowl me away. Felt her unlatch,
A small mass, rocketing like helium, body
Already a swelling replicate of self.

I could see no verve, no afterburn, no spirit
Lingering, just my empty reaching out:
How the dead can cower on the wing of
A plane or, like a missile, shoot out of sight.

Muffled drum of heart, my lungs, aging boxers
Swelling in a crow storm, hungry as Buck
Mulligan for her words, I chew them now,
Hollow seed pods catching on my tongue,

Those whiskers of good intention: sad
Eliot's jet, as if hoarding, gorging, on pain.

3

Every last vein crammed with absence. Hers
Yours, ours, I must return to the now. Two
Incompatible screens, the pixilated grief,
The polyurethane grief, stuffed, animated,

Shrunken sweaters aping across an abandoned
Gym, Sexton's arms outstretched, smoky
Scotch a glass clinking across the honeyed floor.
I await your return and, with it, futures

Uncorking. Hold tight, spray of time, we don't
Race to death, it comes at us; there is no safety fence.
Once you drop, you walk into the forest as though
You owned it, you turn, wave, inhale black of day,

Exhale sight. Inhale death, exhale life, Ozymandias:
Everything that lives is light and she is now dark.

4

Time, they say, time, and with it healing but also
Recrimination and upset, my tumourette an airbag
Behind my eyes, blind me, my lack of patience:
Why is my exuberance rewarded? Hers snuffed?

Siblings crumble slow, unremarkable
As fences across the prairie. Who set the bar

So low? Who has tagged her foot? Mine?
Those red lines traced across a chest,

A lung split open: hard pebbles of light
Pelt your ease. Those high-wire walkers vibrating
In the pain know something of loss's
Hammer, a persistent drum kit open under

The eave where pincers crack
A fly skull.

5

She is everywhere, the widening screen,
A surge in the weather, pages blooming,
Lines with animal movements, useless stalking.
I stare into the soup, trying to ignite some memory

Of eating. Sweet rain where Raven, carrying summer
Storms, stomps the air: a bull, head ready to draw
The sky closed. The more death we know the closer
We are, and yes, the onward path, packed with guilt

And smart knots where pleasures show. I go to
August with her horses, to the clover path under
the power lines. There is no traceable reaction to
The arbutus's shedding while all else blooms, we

Upswing and trill, tunnel our emotions. No more death
Please: bite hard, I want to feel the future coming.

6

I felt something snap just now. It wasn't your parting
Your body – it's months after that, as if all this time
Grief has been spinning out heels and now we slow, steady,
Let it nestle into a fold with the lost coins and lint.

Where you were, the sawed-off limbs of a birch, a scorch
Of concrete, a hemline, shoulders wedged, socks like muffins
Oozing out of jeans, fashion is also exhausted, and who
Cares about whims, please save me from abstraction.

Who will sort the apples? Leonard. Leonard will sort the
Apples. Frederick will drive the car. Jack will feel for you.
Describing is owning. Give me a woman with a lens
In her hand. Give me a woman with a will to read.

Give a woman a lost woman, an open vista, a stack of vellum,
Give me Time, give me swagger, give me your ears.

7

All the gods know is destinations. I have raised
A glass, my eye, your hook. Let's face it, the world
Is a shrinking place and hungry: too much grief
To feed. I float away from you on hard

Covers. I step out on the stacked hours. Words
If they were soil, I would throw them back into the
Compost pile and wait for spring. Those 'this is how
It is' speeches appear and later diamonds soft as bullets.

I went to the library looking to scaffold my thoughts.
Sure, now you say Lucretius. Intelligence is so often
Hindsight. Outside Holly Golightly's townhouse
There are taxis. The end of me, or you, is of no concern.

Frederick Seidel anoints me with the head of his penis.
It is soft as a chamois and spreads like egg across my scalp.

"The Dead Ones"

In the centre of any city the dead ones assemble. On Main Street, under overpasses, by train tracks, the dead lament and rejoice like spiny kites locked to subway wheels. *Me*, they say, spiking through the exhausted air, *watch me*.

The noise you hear when diving into a civic pool is the om of the dead. The humming silence is their slow, methodical dance. The dead have no weight but they stomp nonetheless. They hold hands in long lines; they are determined to be heard, to be seen: *look at me*, the say, diving in and out of the earth like porpoises, *look at me*.

The dead are not firewood. They cannot be collected, ordered or made useful to the living.

In small western towns and suburbs the dead burn good intentions like small trees trimmed in oil. *Useless*, they say, waving their arms in the air, *useless*. On national holidays the dead stack their regrets and explode them with gusts of wind. Of their childhoods – those who have outlived them – some say that the world appeared to be above them, as if they were small gorillas pulled along on a leash.

The dead cause allergies They laugh when we sneeze. They appear at sunset, their belongings condensed into little origami figures. Like the living, they will not listen; they will not leave their baggage outside the gates and so they circle around, sure of a hidden entrance.

In the centre of the glass forest, my grandmother, and maybe yours, lies in state. It is an ashen affair. Silent. Hollow as the inside of a milk carton. You might have stepped on her there, certainly you drove past, thinking of your beautiful future, and your children's future, and the ideas of the future like automated feet clicking south.

Once, when I could not find her small headstone and circled around a group of people for an unnervingly long time, I realized I was in a movie, and the director was standing on her head.

The dead often have starring roles The dead know how to lead. They know how to carry themselves. The dead have gravitas even thought they float.

.

And of course the dead have a sense of humour. Even the most downtrodden dead. Relieved of their burdens, they think of their struggles and laugh. They lie back in death and hone their wit. They come to you in your panic and bite the soft parts of your feet or tickle your palms, they lay their thoughts in the middle of the sidewalk and laugh. They place mirrors on your desk, or pull your lips like rubber bands.

.

To the dead, anger is like a trampoline, it has bounce. Compassion is their superpower, time their weapon. Strong gusts of wind or bursts of sun flare when they are feeling for you. They follow you around, hoping you will notice them.

.

The dead love spring. They eat daffodils. Rocks. Air. Just for the sport of it. They could have felt this way always, even when they lived in a trailer, surrounded by crackheads, or in a quiet suburb surrounded by thick clouds of BBQ, or in their small flats, stacked neatly by the lake, but now, their skin hung out to dry and the clouds so favourable, they lean into the breeze.

A dead one reaches across the table and sticks her tongue down Lee Miller's throat.

Flowers pile up for the dead. Cups of carnations, seafoam rafts of lilies. Every city has a different variety of cemetery flower.

Committed mourners love the hearty chrysanthemum, the geranium, the burning bush, the wisteria, the weeping juniper.

In the north they wait for the spring to bury their dead. They stack them on ice.

Of an afternoon the dead gather by the town clock and mock the living.

A riderless horse follows the procession.

A lone man playing the bagpipe.

Black boots span the road like spilled beetles.

Death's harsh footfalls.

Death in her steel toes.

They still desire, many of them, and so hang on wind currents peering down and yearning.

They say we die as we lived, but I don't believe that. I would like death without judgment. The beheaded know what it is like to lose one's cool. The afterlife does not descend like a bamboo sheet. It may fall, a solid wall of nothing, but I can't imagine someone sorting as the bodies tumble in, like peas for winter, the dark, the sweet, the tainted, rolling into the compost of eternity.

.

Where is she, Lee Miller, what city does she haunt?

.

The sound of death is like sand in my ear; the texture, like bits of bone fragment in the sauce.

.

Death, in her boa, hisses at me on the stairs at night. Death will not let me sleep.

Death and her twin sister, Death.

.

Still, I honour the dead ones. I carry them in boxes, placed on my shelf, under my bed.

I gather pieces of them and carry them on airplanes, I file them, order them, I sew them into the hem of my coat to keep them close.

.

How can we move forward not carrying the weight of our dead?

How can we move forward not carrying the weight of our dead?

When we dead awaken, sure, or let them sleep in our poems, cocooned in chenille or silk. She knees, she curls, she cowering under the antlers of the felled fir, face down, burrowing into the past, kicking the surf of rotting cedar at the future, fanning bright and sudden as lichen, once you see it there on the stone walk, on the forest floor, on the tree, on the bark everywhere like glaciers receding.

In the morning, she sleepwalks through the forest, trying to think of a future, crisp as asteroids, or worse, an atom, needing only to come inside her and split, and she is so hungry to be split, to be entered and torn apart.

The past is knowable, or so she likes to think, but no, no, she knows it isn't so, the path with its spiral of revelations. She elbows, she knees locked, tongue parted, spit, not letting anything inside or out, she a sack of sadness, a lost limb in search of a body.

Why awaken now?

Even Keats, the virgin poet, is asleep.

Anne Carson is a footnote in the biography of death. Few of us get a mention.

The Giantess has split her womb. The city has long ago sold its future. My loved ones like a dandelion to the wind. I have everything to live for and nowhere to be.

The dead know this. They are constantly tying a thread around your ankle. They attach bells to your hair.

EMOTION FRAME
DIMENSIONS

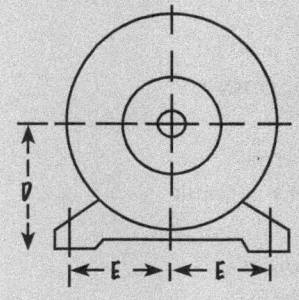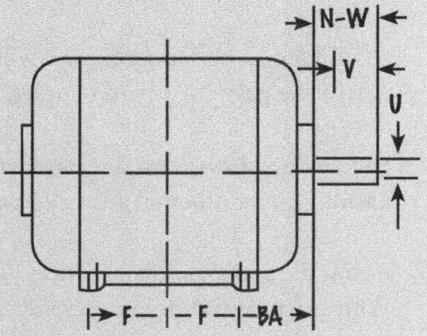

D Circumference of head   E Left and right hemisphere
N–W Parallel processors   V Volume of feeling
                    U Circumference of neuron

"Sylvia Plath's Elegy for Sylvia Plath"

If you can't feel love in life you won't feel it in death, nor
Will you feel the tulip's skin, not the soft gravel

Of childhood under cheek. You will have writhed
Across the page for a hard couplet, a firm rime, ass

High as any downward dog, and cutlass arms
Lashing any mother who tries to pass: let's be frank

About the cost of spurs, mothers like peonies
Whirling in storm drains, families sunk before

Reaching open water. The empty boudoir
Will haunt, but not how you imagine it will.

Nothing, not even death, frees mothers
From the cutting board, the balloons, their

Lack of resistance, *Thoughts*, he said, *quick*
As tulips staggering across the quad.

She heard, *I like my women splayed*
Out, red. Read swollen, domesticated,

Wanting out. The tulips were never warm,
My loves, they never smelled of spring,

They never marked the path out of loneliness,
Never led me home, nor to me, nor away

From what spring, or red, or tulips
Could never be.

"Elegy for a Lost Brother"

But come, my friend,
tell us your own story now, and tell it truly.
Where have your rovings forced you?
What lands of men have you seen, *what sturdy towns,*
what men themselves? Who were *wild, savage,* lawless?
Who were friendly to strangers, god-fearing men? Tell me,
why do you *Weep* and *grieve* so *sorely*: when you hear
the fate for the Argives, hear the fall of Troy?
That is *the gods'* work, *spinning threads of death*
through the lives of mortal men...   650

"Elegy for the Letter Q as It Appears in *The Waves*"

No question, it was the quality of the quadrangles quailed with queues (in quads) that no queen – queer or not – would have sufficient qualities to (quarter or no) quarrel her way through. Though quarrelling might be thought common, a quest among quirky and quizzical quartets, it was actually quite uncommon. Quietly she quivered in a quicksilver quarto of quoits. She was quickest, at least quicker, and she quarreled, quenched and in quotations, finally, quizzically, quit.

"Elegy Written in a City Cemetery"

Somebody left the world last night, and last, and last, and last:[1] wild is the glower[2] of wind, and words too thin, too meek to shelter.[3] *Lament in rhyme*, she says, *lament in roses*:[4] he *was*, and *is* not![5] It will always be darker soon, colder,[6] you who are part anger who bent down in winter,[7] know that your prayers cannot dismiss the darting shade.[8] No, let us not shit upon the ground[9] near the lone pine with ivy overspread,[10] and let me not your giddiness flatten,[11] for so fine the season, so serene the hour[12] and all I have left of that moment is this torn scrap.[13]

I weave my bones thru the freeway haze at Rincon,[14] the self returns again, my natal self:[15] what you see is the red-shouldered[16] judge of the Quirky and Dead. I am not[17] man, man is death, and the world pain.[18] We were all uncountable stars then:[19] the tilt of earth is beautiful[20] from every angle.

I mourn for Adonis[21] – I expected her to look more dead in the casket.[22] Let them bury your big eyes,[23] Death, be not loud; your hand did not give her this blow, she was borne to church on glasses of Grey Goose:[24] Only the bottle knows she is gone.[25] Damn the snow,[26] an uneven basin to stroll:[27] the curfew tolls the knell of closing time.[28] The moon still sends its abundant light.[29] It is a hard time among these stones,[30] for all the toppled, liquid graves.[31] A slumber did your spirit steal.[32] At Wilshire and Santa Monica an opossum crossed.[33] I thought, *Two forms move among the dead, high sleep*[34] *so prescient your absence.*[35]

Small is the poet's needle, God knows:[36] but inside the heart[37] a broken night advances in its glass.[38] Death knelt

among the[39] starving children on your plate:[40] I sometimes
think of those pale, perfect faces[41] who die as cattle, and
I cannot sleep.[42]

The city you graced was swift.[43] Now that the Summer
of Love has become the milk of tunnels;[44] now that the
chestnut candles burn,[45] so may the trees extend their
spreading.[46] There is blessing in this gentle breeze.[47] What
need of bells to mark our loss?[48] Shall I go force an elegy?[49]
The dead sing *Turn the lights down sweetly*.[50] No more for
us the little sighing, nor the grand.[51] All the new thinking
is still about loss.[52]

1 Olga Broumas, 'Elegy.'
2 George Gordon Byron, 'On the Death of a Young Lady, Cousin to the Author, and Very Dear to Him.'
3 John Donne, 'Elegie.'
4 Robert Burns, 'Poor Mailie's Elegy.'
5 Elizabeth Barrett Browning, 'Stanzas on the Death of Lord Byron.'
6 Marvin Bell, 'An Elegy for the Past.'
8 T. S. Eliot, 'Elegy,' *The Waste Land*.
9 Lawrence Ferlinghetti, 'An Elegy to Dispel Gloom: After the Assassinations of Mayor George Moscone of San Francisco and City Supervisor Harvey Milk November 27, 1978.'
10 Samuel Taylor Coleridge, 'Elegy Imitated from One of Akenside's Blank-Verse Inscriptions.'
11 Charles Christopher Bowen, 'Sappho's Last Elegy.'
12 Francis Douglas, 'A Pastoral Elegy.'
13 Larry Levis, 'Elegy Ending in the Sound of a Skipping Rope.'
14 Tom Clark, 'Little Elegy For Bob Marley (D. 5/11/81).'
15 Jane Austen, 'To the Memory of Mrs. Lefroy.'
16 Eavan Boland, 'On the Gift of *The Birds Of America* By John James Audubon.'
17 John Danforth, 'A Funeral Elegy Humbly Dedicated to the Renowned Memory of the Honorable Thomas Danforth, Esq.'
18 John Donne, 'Elegy on the Lady Markham.'
19 Larry Levis, 'Elegy with an Angel at its Gate.'
20 Ian McMillan, 'Elegy for an Hour of Daylight.'
21 Elizabeth Barrett Browning, 'A Lament For Adonis.'
22 Richard Hugo, 'Elegy.'
23 Edna St. Vincent Millay, 'Elegy.'
24 Margaret Cavendish, Duchess of Newcastle, 'An Elegy.'
25 Sara Teasdale, 'Dark of the Moon.'

[26] Yusef Komunyakaa, 'Elegy For Thelonious.'

[27] Sandra McPherson, 'Elegy for Floating Things.'

[28] Thomas Gray, 'Elegy Written in a Country Churchyard.'

[29] Langston Hughes, 'To a Dead Friend.'

[30] Greg Glazner, 'Summer Elegy in Santa Fe.'

[31] Henry King, 'An Elegy upon Mrs. Kirk Unfortunately Drowned In Thames.'

[32] William Wordsworth, 'A Slumber Did My Spirit Seal.'

[33] Larry Levis, 'The Oldest Living Thing in L.A.'

[34] Wallace Stevens, 'The Owl in the Sarcophagus.'

[35] May Sarton, 'Elegy.'

[36] Peter Pindar, 'Elegy to a Friend.'

[37] Judith Goldman, 'proportions of a giant in monument valley.'

[38] Muriel Rukeyser, 'Second Elegy. Age of Magicians.'

[39] William Wordsworth, 'She Dwelt Among the Untrodden Ways.'

[40] Ben Lerner, 'Mad Lib Elegy.'

[41] Wilfred Owen, 'The One Remains.'

[42] Wilfred Owen, 'Anthem for Doomed Youth.'

[43] Marilyn Hacker, 'Elegy for a Soldier.'

[44] Larry Levis, 'Elegy for Whatever Had a Pattern in It.'

[45] Jon Stallworthy, 'Elegy for a Mis-Spent Youth.'

[46] Tibullus, 'To Priapus: Elegies 1.iv,' trans. John Dart.

[47] William Wordsworth, *The Prelude*.

[48] William Wordsworth, 'Composed on the Eve of the Marriage of a Friend in the Vale of Grasmere.'

[49] John Donne, 'An Elegy on Mrs. Bulstrode.'

[50] Terrance Hayes, 'Stick Elegy.'

[51] Ezra Pound, 'Threnos.'

[52] Robert Hass, 'Meditation at Lagunitas.'

Afterword: "Lyric Conceptualism, A Manifesto in Progress"

The Lyric Conceptualist has moved beyond the indigestible and the unreadable, in fact, beyond all gestures that have made pleasure the enemy of reading.

Still, the Lyric Conceptualist remains true to her politics of inclusion, appreciating the thinkership of conceptual poetry, the revelations in mass assemblages that concretize the ephemeral textuality of daily life. Yet she stubbornly continues to bask in the reverie of solitude.

Lyric Conceptualism indulges in the excess of language while appreciating the clean lines of the minimal.

Lyric Conceptualism does not confuse clarity with simplicity.

Lyric Conceptualism rejects naïve notions of truth and beauty.

Lyric Conceptualism is not simply expressionism.

Lyric Conceptualism does not accept that content does not matter and still appreciates the way that content does not always matter.

If the Lyric Conceptualist lives in a forest it may be a concrete one, or a forest planted and coiffed by humans as much as animals, though she is not ready for the merely virtual or textual.

The Lyric Conceptualist likely has one foot in the gallery and one foot on the earth. She can make the distinction between floor and ground. She knows a book and how to read one in myriad forms.

Lyric Conceptualism understands that insight and revelation are difficult to come by no matter how the poem has been conceived.

Lyric Conceptualism suggests that to argue for the death of anything is not really that interesting.

Lyric Conceptualism accepts the tension between the self and the poetic subject, wrestling always with the desire to give over to the poem and to be the poet in the poem.

The Lyric Conceptualist looks longingly at those who enjoy the benefits of community but turns away from the gated community.

Lyric Conceptualism is a voyeuristic mode.

Lyric Conceptualism is informed, not enslaved, by theory.

Are you writing it or is it writing you?

Does the form evolve or constrain?

Is your poetry always already written?

Are your ideas always already thought?

Lyric Conceptualism accepts appropriation and re-contextualization as useful, if not essential gestures but does not confine her process to these gestures.

The Lyric Conceptualist does not buy that an abandoned constraint constitutes failure.

On the other hand, the Lyric Conceptualist looks to where she is acquiring her content.

Mud is mud is mud, or the thinking of a poem is the poem.

On the other hand, density does not necessarily lead to complexity and found language is not necessarily more interesting than mined language.

Many conceptual poets are models for Lyric Conceptualism.

Many Language poets are models for Lyric Conceptualism.

Many lyric poets are models for Lyric Conceptualism.

Lyric Conceptualism, then, is not new.

Lyric Conceptualism is not bound to appropriation. It is not bound to indoors. Or to the archive, though it often originates there. It is not bound to mind alone, nor is it bound to chat rooms or search engines, though again, it often originates there.

The Lyric Conceptualist acknowledges her debts to multiple strands of contemporary poetics, art, design, architecture, philosophy, environmentalism, unions, students, modernism, postmodernism, conceptualism and romanticism.

The Lyric Conceptualist is a master of collision, she is not afraid of entering into other texts.

The Lyric Conceptualist is not necessarily a feminine body, but it has the stink of the impure, a certain irreverence for the master, therefore it is by default, feminine in construction.

Lyric Conceptualism is as much WalMart as Zaha Hadid as suburbia and Andrea Zittel.

Lyric Conceptualism is a poetics of the sentence, but it does not turn its back on the relationship between words, nor the power of prosody, nor the possibility of lyric propulsion. On the other hand, nor does Lyric Conceptualism shy away from the knotted and the complex.

Lyric Conceptualism imagines herself a boat, fluid, without handles, able to slip through definitions, anchor at will.

Lyric Conceptualism is interested in achieving the sculptural.

Lyric Conceptualism is comfortable existing outside of dominant narratives. In fact Lyric Conceptualism makes good use of cast off texts and remains of genius.

Lyric Conceptualism is unable to turn away from the problems of the earth and yet committed to thinking through the way we think about the problems of the earth. Yes, Lyric Conceptualism still believes in world.

To that end Lyric Conceptualism doesn't shy away from being used as a protest tool and is not adverse to being occupied or called to action.

The Lyric Conceptualist is most often a spectator, though not necessarily in retreat.

The Lyric Conceptualist is an excessive elegist.

The Lyric Conceptualist is a trough that catches the excess, the off cuts, the remnants, the offal of language.

Lyric Conceptualism is interested in fun but not wedded only to the ironic, the distant and mocking.

Lyric Conceptualism's goal is to create openings rather than closures. It offers itself as a courtyard, stadium, meadow, and variously, a reclaimed parking lot, a battlefield made food co-op, a factory turned performance space, a transitional space, reclaimed land, an idea with no end.

—*Sina Queyras*

Acknowledgements

Erin Wunker would like to thank Sina Queyras for her work, words, and world-making, and Bart Vautour and Elizabeth Bea for making worlds with me.

   We are grateful to the publishers of the following works for permission to reprint. Afterword originally published on *Harriet the Blog*, the Poetry Foundation Blog.

Slip (Toronto: ECW, 2001)
"Scrabbling"

Teethmarks (Roberts Creek, BC: Nightwood, 2004)
From *Jersey Fragments*
        "Me Victorious"
From *Dizzy, or, My Mother's Life as Cindy Sherman*
        "TV M/other"
        "Roadside Memory #1"

Lemon Hound (Toronto: Coach House, 2006)
From *A river by the moment*
        "The river is all thumbs"
        "Whose genealogy?"
        "If only"
        "If"
From *On the scent*
        "1."
        "4."
        "5."
From *Virginia, Vanessa, the strands*
        "There was the moment of the puddle in the path"
From *Meanwhile, elsewhere, otherwise*
        "Some other poets and the puddle"
From The Waves, *an unmaking*
        "...*The Waves*, an architecture"

Expressway (Toronto: Coach House, 2009)
From *The Endless Path of the New*
    "A Memorable Fancy"
From *Some Moments From a Land Before the Expressway*
    "Lines Written Many Miles from Grasmere" 1, 4, 14
From *The Endless Hum*
    "Murmurings, Movements or Fringe Manifesto"

Proverbs of Hell

MxT (Toronto: Coach House, 2014)
"Alternate Mourning"
"Water, Water Everywhere"
"Dear One"
"Like a Jet"
"The Dead Ones"
"Emotion Frame Dimensions"
"Sylvia Plath's Elegy for Sylvia Plath"
"Elegy for a Lost Brother"
"Elegy for the Letter Q as It Appears in *The Waves*"
"Elegy Written in a City Cemetery"

M. Travis Lane *The Crisp Day Closing on My Hand: The Poetry of M. Travis Lane*, edited by Jeanette Lynes, with an afterword by M. Travis Lane • 2007 • xvi + 86 pp. • ISBN 978-1-55458-025-5

Tim Lilburn *Desire Never Leaves: The Poetry of Tim Lilburn*, edited by Alison Calder, with an afterword by Tim Lilburn • 2007 • xiv + 50 pp. • ISBN 978-0-88920-514-7

Eli Mandel *From Room to Room: The Poetry of Eli Mandel*, edited by Peter Webb, with an afterword by Andrew Stubbs • 2011 • xviii + 66 pp. • ISBN 978-1-55458-255-6

Daphne Marlatt *Rivering: The Poetry of Daphne Marlatt*, edited by Susan Knutson, with an afterword by Daphne Marlatt • 2014 • xxiv + 72 pp. • ISBN 978-1-77112-038-8

Steve McCaffery *Verse and Worse: Selected and New Poems of Steve McCaffery 1989–2009*, edited by Darren Wershler, with an afterword by Steve McCaffery • 2010 • xiv + 76 pp. • ISBN 978-1-55458-188-7

Don McKay *Field Marks: The Poetry of Don McKay*, edited by Méira Cook, with an afterword by Don McKay • 2006 • xxvi + 60 pp. • ISBN 978-0-88920-494-2

Al Purdy *The More Easily Kept Illusions: The Poetry of Al Purdy*, edited by Robert Budde, with an afterword by Russell Brown • 2006 • xvi + 80 pp. • ISBN 978-0-88920-490-4

Sina Queyras *Barking & Biting: The Poetry of Sina Queyras*, edited by Erin Wunker, with an afterword by Sina Queyras • 2016 • xviii + 68 pp. • ISBN 978-1-77112-216-0

F.R. Scott *Leaving the Shade of the Middle Ground: The Poetry of F.R. Scott*, edited by Laura Moss, with an afterword by George Elliott Clarke • 2011 • xxiv + 72 pp. • ISBN 978-1-55458-367-6

Fred Wah *The False Laws of Narrative: The Poetry of Fred Wah*, edited by Louis Cabri, with an afterword by Fred Wah • 2009 • xxiv + 78 pp. • ISBN 978-1-555458-046-0

Tom Wayman *The Order in Which We Do Things: The Poetry of Tom Wayman*, edited by Owen Percy, with an afterword by Tom Wayman • 2014 + xx + 92 pp. • ISBN 978-1-55458-995-1

Jan Zwicky *Chamber Music: The Poetry of Jan Zwicky*, edited by Darren Bifford and Warren Heiti, with an interview with Jan Zwicky • 2015 • xx + 82 pp. • ISBN 978-1-77112-091-3